W9-DAK-665

chicken

chicken

TIME
LIFE
BOOKS

Alexandria, Virginia

TIME® LIFE BOOKS

Time-Life Books is a division of Time Life Inc.
Time-Life is a trademark of Time Warner Inc. and affiliated companies.

TIME LIFE INC.
CHAIRMAN AND CHIEF EXECUTIVE OFFICER: Jim Nelson
PRESIDENT AND CHIEF OPERATING OFFICER: Steven Janas

TIME-LIFE BOOKS
PRESIDENT: Larry Jellen
VICE PRESIDENT AND PUBLISHER: Neil S. Levin
VICE PRESIDENT, CONTENT DEVELOPMENT: Jennifer L. Pearce
SENIOR SALES DIRECTOR: Richard J. Vreeland
DIRECTOR, MARKETING AND PUBLICITY: Inger Forland
DIRECTOR OF TRADE SALES: Dana Hobson
DIRECTOR OF CUSTOM PUBLISHING: John Lalor
DIRECTOR OF RIGHTS AND LICENSING: Olga Vezeris
DIRECTOR OF NEW PRODUCT DEVELOPMENT: Carolyn M. Clark
EXECUTIVE EDITOR: Linda Bellamy
DIRECTOR OF DESIGN: Kate L. McConnell
TECHNICAL SPECIALIST: Monika Lynde

CHICKEN
PROJECT EDITOR: Paula York-Soderlund
DESIGN ASSISTANT: Jody Billert

First published in the U.K. in 1999 by Hamlyn
Octopus Publishing Group Limited, 2–4 Heron Quays, London E14 4JP

Printed in China.
10 9 8 7 6 5 4 3 2 1

School and library distribution by Time-Life Education, P.O. Box 85026, Richmond, Virginia 23285-5026.

Library of Congress Cataloging-in-Publication Data
Chicken : over 60 simple recipes for great home cooking!
        p. cm.
    Includes index.
    ISBN 0-7370-2064-4 (hardcover)
        1. Cookery (Chicken) I. Time-Life Books.

    TX750.5.C45 C456 2001
    641.6'65--dc21   00-051187

Notes
1 Milk should be whole milk unless otherwise stated.
2 Fresh herbs should be used unless otherwise stated. If unavailable, use dried herbs as an alternative but only half the amount stated.
3 Pepper should be freshly ground black pepper unless otherwise stated; season to taste.
4 Do not refreeze a dish that has been frozen previously.
5 Chiles range from hot, medium, to mild. Use according to taste.

 APR - - 2002

Fabulous finger foods, elegant salads, and light but sustaining soups are among the dishes featured here. Tempt your guests with chili chicken drumsticks, smoked chicken & citrus salad, honeyed chicken wings, or chicken & corn soup.

A collection of delicious and deceptively simple recipes for those days when you have no time to plan an elaborate menu or hours to spend in the kitchen, yet want fresh home-cooked food rather than take-out food.

Chicken has world-wide appeal; this chapter features many diverse styles of cooking. The choice includes Burmese chicken curry & cellophane noodles, Tex-Mex chicken with salsa, Moroccan tagine, and Italian roast chicken.

The dishes in this chapter range from an impressive chicken galantine to serve at a cold buffet, to a mouthwatering, Indian-inspired, spiced, roast chicken. Serve them when you want to impress friends and family with something out of the ordinary.

contents

introduction

Chicken is one of the most popular of all savory foods – quick, versatile and easy to cook – and suitable for both simple and sophisticated dishes, as this wide-ranging collection of recipes shows. It is also a favorite all over the world, and chicken dishes can be found stamped with every national style and choice of flavorings.

The best chickens are free-range birds, but these are more expensive than regular chickens. Factory-farmed chicken comes in several varieties, including corn-fed chickens, which have creamy yellow flesh from the corn they eat. The cheapest birds are those found in the freezer section of supermarkets. These do not have the flavor of fresh birds but are nutritious and useful for making stock.

Whole Chickens

Whole chickens can weigh anything from 1 lb. for the smallest cornish game hens, one of which makes an individual serving, to huge 8 lb. roasters, which can be served as an alternative to the Christmas turkey. Broilers, which are up to 12 weeks old and weigh around 2½ lbs., will feed 2–3 people. When choosing a chicken, look for a bird with a plump white breast, smooth and pliable legs, and moist but not wet skin which is free of dark patches and has not split. Whole chickens can be roasted, pot-roasted, poached, braised, or steamed.

Chicken Pieces

Cut-up chicken is sold as quarters (including leg and breast meat, with bones in), breasts, thighs, and drumsticks. Thighs and drumsticks are good for stews and barbecuing. Breasts are available with and without bones and skin. The latter is sometimes labeled as fillet. All types of breast meat are top quality lean meat and cook very quickly. Use them for pan-frying, grilling, poaching, steaming, stir-frying, and sautéing. Chicken livers are sold in tubs in the refrigerated and freezer sections of supermarkets.

Chicken & Health

Raw poultry contains low levels of bacteria, including salmonella, which cause food poisoning, but correct storage and handling will render the bacteria harmless. When you get a fresh chicken home, remove the plastic bag and styrofoam tray, and put the chicken in the refrigerator on a plate, covered loosely with foil or plastic. If you have bought a chicken with giblets, remove them from the chicken, and store them separately in a covered bowl. A fresh chicken should be cooked and eaten within two days.

'A bird in the hand is the best way to eat chicken.'

Anonymous

A frozen chicken should be put in the freezer as soon as you get it home. It should be thawed in the refrigerator before cooking, so that no ice crystals remain. Do not attempt to thaw chicken by putting it into hot water since this will make it tough. Never refreeze thawed raw chicken.

Chicken is a boon to weight watchers as it is low in fat and cholesterol. To reduce the fat content still further, remove the skin before cooking, but bear in mind that the skin helps keep the bird moist during cooking, so you may want to leave the skin on for cooking but remove it before serving.

Hands, utensils, and work surfaces must be scrupulously clean before preparing chicken, or any other poultry, and raw and cooked poultry should never be prepared at the same time. Before cooking, always wipe raw poultry with paper towels, wiping also the cavities of whole birds, which may harbor bacteria.

To test that a whole chicken is cooked, insert a skewer or fork into the thickest part of the thigh. If the juices are clear, the chicken is cooked. Any hint of pinkness means that further cooking is needed.

Chicken Stock
A well-flavored chicken stock is at the heart of many chicken recipes. Store-bought stock cubes tend to be salty, and although there are good, ready-made, chicken stocks sold in the chilled section of supermarkets these days, there is no substitute for a homemade version. The chicken stock on page 9 may be made with the uncooked bones and trimmings, when you have cut-up or boned a chicken, or with the leftover carcass after cooking. It will keep in the refrigerator for 3 days. Otherwise, you can store it in a freezer for up to 3 months. To save space, boil the stock until it is reduced and concentrated, and then freeze it in an ice-cube tray. The frozen concentrated stock cubes can then be stored in a plastic bag in the freezer. When you need a chicken stock cube, simply put a frozen stock cube into a little hot liquid and stir to dissolve.

chef's salad ●
chicken & corn soup ●
chicken liver pâté ●
chili chicken drumsticks ●
chicken & leek soup ●
honeyed chicken wings ●
chicken & raisin salad ●
chicken & ham phyllo wraps ●
marinated chicken kebabs ●
parmesan chicken drumsticks ●
steamed chicken dumplings ●
stir-fried lemon chicken with vegetables ●
club sandwich ●
smoked chicken & citrus salad ●
chicken & avocado salad ●

small
courses

chef's salad

1 First make the dressing. Put all the ingredients into a screwtop jar and shake vigorously until thoroughly combined.

2 Tear the lettuce into bite-sized pieces and place them in a large salad bowl, along with the mixed herb sprigs. Toss together lightly.

3 Add all the remaining ingredients except the dressing, and combine. Add salt and pepper to taste, and lightly toss the salad.

4 Just before serving, spoon the dressing over the salad, and toss lightly.

1 small lettuce (e.g. butterhead, red oakleaf, escarole, chicory), separated into leaves

small handful of mixed herb sprigs

1 cucumber, thinly sliced

¼ cup walnut pieces

about ½ lb. cooked chicken, diced

about 4 slices ham, cut into strips (to yield 1 cup)

¾ cup crumbled cheese (e.g. Edam, Emmental or Swiss, sharp Cheddar)

handful of seedless grapes, cut in half (optional)

salt and pepper

French Dressing:

2 tablespoons red or white wine vinegar

1–2 garlic cloves, crushed

2 teaspoons Dijon mustard

¼ teaspoon sugar

6 tablespoons olive oil

salt and pepper

Serves 4

Preparation time: 20 minutes

chicken & corn soup

1 Pour the stock into a large pot and add 1 cup of the corn. Bring to a boil, add salt and pepper to taste, cover, and simmer for 15 minutes.

2 Pour the soup into a food processor or blender and blend until smooth, then return it to the pot. Reheat the soup. If it is not thick enough for your liking, blend the cornstarch with the water to make a thin paste, stir it into the soup, and bring to a boil, stirring. Add the remaining corn and the reserved chopped chicken, and simmer for 5 minutes.

3 Taste, and adjust the seasoning before serving, and garnish with the diced red pepper and strips.

1 quart Chicken Stock (see page 9), with a little of the cooked chicken reserved and chopped

1½ cups corn

2 teaspoons cornstarch (optional)

1 tablespoon water (optional)

salt and pepper

red bell pepper, diced and cut into strips, for garnishing

Serves 4
Preparation time: 10 minutes
Cooking time: 20–25 minutes

1 Melt the butter in a large frying pan. Add the bacon, garlic, and onion, and cook gently for 3 minutes. Stir in the chicken livers and cook for 5 minutes. Season liberally with salt and pepper. Stir in the herbs and mushrooms. Add the sherry and cook until the liquid has evaporated. Let cool, then blend in a food processor or blender until smooth. Stir in the cream and the lemon juice.

2 Spoon the pâté into a greased ovenproof dish. Cover with a lid, and set the dish in a roasting pan filled with 1 inch of water. Bake in a preheated oven at 300°F for 2–2½ hours, until cooked through. Let cool, then cover and chill until needed.

3 Garnish the pâté with watercress, and serve with hot toast or French bread.

1 stick (½ cup) butter

½ lb. Canadian bacon, chopped

4 garlic cloves, crushed

2 small onions, chopped

2 lbs. chicken livers, chopped

4 thyme sprigs

4 parsley sprigs

½ lb. white mushrooms, chopped (about 2⅓ cups)

½ cup dry sherry

½ cup heavy cream

2 teaspoons lemon juice

salt and pepper

watercress sprigs or small arugula leaves, for garnishing

Serves 12

Preparation time: 20 minutes

Cooking time: 2¼–2¾ hours

chicken liver pâté

■ This flavorsome pâté will keep well in the refrigerator for at least a week.

chili chicken drumsticks

1 Heat the oil in a frying pan and fry the onion and garlic until soft and lightly colored. Add the ketchup, Worcestershire sauce, chili seasoning, vinegar, jam, and mustard, and bring slowly to a boil. Simmer gently for 2 minutes, then remove the pan from the heat and let cool.

2 Arrange the drumsticks in a shallow dish in a single layer and pour the sauce over them. Cover, and let marinate in a cool place for at least 3 hours, turning the drumsticks occasionally.

3 Drain the marinade from the drumsticks and set aside. Put the drumsticks under a preheated medium broiler and cook for about 8–10 minutes on each side until they are cooked through and well browned. Put them on a warmed platter, and garnish with parsley sprigs.

4 Put the reserved marinade into a saucepan, bring to the boil and cook for 2–3 minutes to heat through thoroughly. Serve with the drumsticks.

2 tablespoons oil

1 onion, finely chopped

1 garlic clove, crushed

⅔ cup ketchup

3 tablespoons Worcestershire sauce

2–3 teaspoons chili seasoning

⅔ cup red wine vinegar

2–3 tablespoons apricot jam

1 teaspoon mustard powder

20 chicken drumsticks

parsley sprigs, for garnishing

Serves 10
Preparation time: 20 minutes, plus marinating
Cooking time: about 20 minutes

1 Put the chicken in a large pot, and add the lemon zest, onion, carrots, and celery. Pour in the water to cover, then add the bouquet garni, and salt and pepper to taste. Bring to a boil over a medium heat. Lower the heat, cover, and simmer for 1½ hours or until the chicken is tender and the juices run clear when the thickest part of a thigh is pierced with a fork.

2 Lift the chicken out of the liquid and leave until cool enough to handle. Remove and discard the lemon zest and bouquet garni.

3 Meanwhile, add the leeks to the liquid in the pan and simmer, uncovered, over medium heat for 10 minutes or until just tender. Remove the chicken meat from the bones, and discard all skin and fat. Cut the meat into bite-sized pieces.

4 Crumble the stock cubes in a bowl, add the egg yolk and cream, and stir well to mix. Add a few spoonfuls of the hot soup liquid and stir well again, then whisk this mixture gradually back into the soup. Add the chicken and simmer over a gentle heat, stirring constantly, for about 5 minutes until the chicken is heated through and the soup has thickened slightly.

5 Remove the soup from the heat and stir in the grated lemon zest and parsley. Taste for seasoning and serve at once.

a 4-lb. roasting chicken, giblets removed

thinly sliced zest of 1 lemon

1 onion, thinly sliced

3 carrots, thinly sliced

2 celery stalks, thinly sliced

2–2½ quarts water

1 large bouquet garni

3 leeks, trimmed, cleaned, and thickly sliced

1–2 chicken stock cubes, according to taste (optional)

1 egg yolk

¼ cup heavy cream

salt and pepper

finely grated zest of 1 lemon

2 tablespoons finely chopped parsley

Serves 4–6

Preparation time: 20 minutes

Cooking time: about 1¾ hours

chicken & leek soup

honeyed chicken wings

1 To make the marinade, mix together all the ingredients in a bowl, mixing thoroughly until combined. Put the chicken wings into a shallow bowl and pour the marinade on top. Spread the marinade all over them, then cover, and leave in a cool place for 2 hours.

2 Meanwhile, make the sauce. Heat the oil in a small saucepan and fry the onion for about 5 minutes until golden brown. Stir in the sugar, lime juice, and peanut butter, and then add the coconut cream, a little at a time. Add the salt, and cook over a gentle heat until smooth and thick. Set aside.

3 Remove the chicken wings from the marinade and place them on a rack in a baking tray. Cook in a preheated oven at 375° for 15–20 minutes, until golden brown and cooked through, basting from time to time with any remaining marinade. Otherwise, broil them for 5–7 minutes on each side. Serve with the warm dipping sauce.

12 chicken wings, trimmed

Marinade:

3 tablespoons soy sauce

¼ cup honey

2 tablespoons vinegar

1 tablespoon sherry

2 teaspoons soft brown sugar

½ teaspoon ground ginger

1 garlic clove, crushed

Dipping Sauce:

2 tablespoons olive oil

2 tablespoons grated onion

2 tablespoons brown sugar

1 teaspoon lime juice

2 tablespoons peanut butter

6 tablespoons coconut cream

pinch of salt

Serves 4

Preparation time: 15 minutes, plus marinating

Cooking time: 20–25 minutes

3 tablespoons raisins

juice of 1 small orange

pinch of ground cloves

1 teaspoon olive oil

⅓ cup slivered almonds

1 lb. cooked chicken, cut into strips

1 head radicchio, shredded

1 small head of lettuce, shredded

1 tablespoon French dressing (see page 13)

salt and pepper

handful of parsley leaves, for garnishing

1 Put the raisins, orange juice, and ground cloves into a small saucepan. Heat until boiling, then remove from the heat and let stand for about 30 minutes to plump the raisins.

2 Heat the oil in a small saucepan over medium heat and brown the almonds, stirring constantly until golden.

3 Put the raisins, almonds, chicken, and shredded salad leaves into a serving bowl. Toss, and season well with salt and pepper. To serve, spoon the dressing over it and scatter with parsley leaves.

Serves 4	
Preparation time: 15 minutes, plus standing	
Cooking time: about 12 minutes	

chicken & raisin salad

1 Split the chicken breasts almost in half horizontally, open them out, and place them between two sheets of plastic wrap. Beat with a rolling pin to flatten them. Arrange the chicken over a large sheet of foil, overlapping the pieces slightly to form an 8 x 10 inch rectangle. Cover evenly with the slices of ham.

2 Heat the oil in a saucepan, add the shallots and fry for about 5 minutes until softened. Remove from the heat and stir in the watercress, feta, lemon juice, and egg, and season with salt and pepper. Mix well. Spread the mixture evenly over the ham to within ½ inch of the edge. Using the foil to help you, roll up the chicken, ham, and filling from one long end. Wrap the foil around the roll and set aside.

3 Mix together the melted butter and mustard. Layer 3 or 4 sheets of phyllo, depending on their thickness, on an oiled baking sheet, brushing each one thinly with the mustard butter. Carefully unwrap the chicken roll from the foil and place it in the center. Arrange 3 more sheets of phyllo dough over the top, brushing each one lightly with mustard butter. Scrunch 2 sheets of phyllo and arrange over the top. Press round the edge to seal the filling, then brush the top with any remaining butter.

4 Bake in a preheated oven at 375°F for 45–50 minutes, until the pastry is crisp and golden brown. Serve warm or cold, cut into thick slices.

1½ lbs. boneless, skinless, chicken breasts

½ lb. sliced cooked ham

1 tablespoon sunflower oil

2 shallots, finely chopped (or 1 small mild onion)

4 oz. watercress – or spinach, if unavailable, chopped (about 2 cups)

4 oz. feta cheese, crumbled (about 1 cup)

1 tablespoon lemon juice

1 egg, beaten

½ stick (¼ cup) butter, melted

2 teaspoons wholegrain mustard

9 oz. package phyllo dough

salt and pepper

Serves 8	
Preparation time: 30 minutes	
Cooking time: 45–50 minutes	

chicken & ham phyllo wraps

marinated chicken kebabs

1 To make the marinade, squeeze the lime or lemon juice into a large bowl and add the honey, chopped chile, and olive oil, and stir until the mixture is well blended and smooth. Add the chicken to the marinade and mix gently until well coated. Cover, and chill for at least 1 hour.

2 Thread the chicken on to pre-soaked wooden skewers and brush with the marinade. Place under a preheated hot broiler, or cook over a barbecue, for 15–20 minutes, turning occasionally, until the chicken is tender and golden brown. Brush the kebabs with more marinade if necessary.

3 Meanwhile, make the avocado sauce. Blend the olive oil and vinegar in a bowl, then beat in the mashed avocado until thick and smooth. Stir in the chopped tomato and scallions, and the sour cream. Serve the kebabs hot, with the avocado sauce and the pomegranate seeds.

6 boneless, skinless chicken breasts, cut into large chunks

seeds of 1 pomegranate, for serving

Marinade:

juice of 2 limes or lemons

1 tablespoon honey

1 green chile, finely chopped

2 tablespoons olive oil

Avocado Sauce:

3 tablespoons olive oil

1 tablespoon red wine vinegar

1 large avocado, peeled, pitted, and mashed

1 large tomato, skinned and chopped

2 scallions, chopped

½ cup sour cream

Serves 4

Preparation time: 15 minutes, plus marinating

Cooking time: 15–20 minutes

1 · Mix the breadcrumbs and Parmesan cheese in a bowl. Season the flour with salt and pepper and sprinkle on a plate. Put the eggs in another bowl.

2 Coat the drumsticks with the seasoned flour, shaking off any excess. Dip them in the egg and roll them in the breadcrumbs. Arrange on a plate, cover, and chill for 30 minutes.

3 Cook the drumsticks under a preheated broiler for 15–20 minutes or until they are cooked through and the juices run clear when pierced with a fork. Serve hot or cold, garnished with rosemary sprigs.

1⅓ cups fresh white breadcrumbs

1 cup finely grated Parmesan cheese

2 tablespoons flour

2 eggs, beaten

8 large chicken drumsticks, skinned

salt and pepper

rosemary sprigs, for garnishing

Serves 4
Preparation time: 15 minutes, plus chilling
Cooking time: 15–20 minutes

parmesan chicken drumsticks

steamed chicken dumplings

1 Sift the flour into a mixing bowl and pour in the water. Mix well to form a dough. Knead for 5 minutes, then place in a bowl, cover with a damp cloth, and leave for 10 minutes.

2 Meanwhile, make the filling. Cut the chicken into small pieces and place in a bowl with the bamboo shoots, scallions, ginger, sugar, soy sauce, sherry, stock, oil, and salt. Mix thoroughly.

3 Cut the dough in half and shape each piece into a long roll. Cut each roll into 16 slices, flatten them into circles, and roll the circles out to make them 3 inches in diameter. Put 1 tablespoon of filling in the center of each circle, gather up the edges, and twist at the top to seal it. Line a steamer with the cabbage leaves. Place the dumplings on the cabbage and steam, covered, for 20 minutes.

4 To make the sauce, pound the garlic, chiles, and sugar using a mortar and pestle. Stir in the lime juice and pulp, nam pla, and water, and mix well. Serve with the dumplings.

4 cups flour

1¼ cups water

1 small cabbage, separated into leaves

Filling:

1 lb. boneless, skinless chicken breasts

8 oz. can bamboo shoots, drained and chopped

3 scallions, finely chopped

3 slices fresh ginger, peeled and finely chopped

2 teaspoons sugar

2 teaspoons light soy sauce

2 tablesoons dry sherry

2 tablespoons Chicken Stock (see page 9)

1 teaspoon sesame oil

salt

Tangy Chile Sauce:

2 garlic cloves

4 dried red chiles or 1 fresh red chile

5 teaspoons sugar

juice and pulp of ¼ lime

¼ cup Thai fish sauce (nam pla) or soy sauce

5 tablespoons water

Serves 8
Preparation time: 45 minutes
Cooking time: 20 minutes

12 oz. boneless, skinless smoked chicken, cut into chunks

1 pink grapefruit

2 small oranges

2 cucumbers, thinly sliced

1 small fennel bulb, trimmed and thinly sliced (optional)

2 oz. chicory (about 1 large handful)

2 oz. corn salad, watercress, or arugula (about 1 large handful)

pink peppercorns (optional)

salt and pepper

Yogurt Dressing:

⅔ cup plain yogurt

1 tablespoon lemon juice

1 teaspoon honey

½ teaspoon Dijon mustard

salt and pepper

Serves 4

Preparation time: 20 minutes

---

1 To make the dressing, put all the ingredients in a small bowl and beat with a wooden spoon until smooth.

2 Put the chicken pieces in a large bowl. Using a small sharp knife, peel the grapefruit and oranges, taking care to remove all the pith. Working over a bowl to catch the juices, break them into segments. Set the juice aside. Add the citrus fruit to the chicken, along with the cucumber and fennel. Toss lightly to combine.

3 Divide the salad greens among four individual plates and arrange the chicken mixture on top. To serve, stir the reserved citrus juices and the pink peppercorns, if using, into the dressing, and pour it over the salad.

smoked chicken & citrus salad

■ This yogurt dressing is low in fat and calories. It can be varied according to taste by adding chopped herbs or pickles, garlic, curry paste, or finely grated orange zest.

chicken & avocado salad

1 Place the chicken in a mixing bowl with the onion, apple, walnuts, and raisins.

2 Add the sliced avocados to the chicken mixture.

3 Mix the dressing ingredients together, pour them over the chicken and avocado mixture, and stir well. Place the salad greens on four plates and top with the chicken and avocado mixture. Serve the salad sprinkled with chopped dill.

■ Smoked or Tandoori chicken can be used instead of plain chicken in this salad, providing a variation in the flavor.

½ lb. boneless, skinless, cooked chicken, shredded

1 small red onion, thinly sliced

1 small red apple, thinly sliced

¼ cup roughly chopped walnuts

1 tablespoon golden raisins

2 avocados, peeled, pitted, and sliced

Dressing:

1 tablespoon French mustard

3 tablespoons olive oil

1 tablespoon white wine vinegar

1 teaspoon sugar

1 garlic clove, crushed

1 teaspoon chopped thyme

For Serving:

1 bag of mixed salad greens

1 tablespoon chopped dill

Serves 4
Preparation time: 5 minutes

chicken pizza mexicana •

spicy chicken casserole •

chicken sautéed with mushrooms •

country chicken with peppers & tomatoes •

chicken & lemon croquettes •

cashew chicken •

hot chicken liver salad •

charbroiled chicken with tomato-chile salsa •

chicken & tomato pasta •

chicken & orange shells •

chicken & pea pasta bake •

pasta with chicken, cream, & mushroom sauce •

chicken with scallions, soy, & celery •

broiled chicken with cheese •

warm salad of chicken & red pepper •

quick & easy

1 Heat the butter with the oil in a large frying pan. Add the chicken livers and cook over high heat for 3–4 minutes, stirring frequently, until browned on the outside but still lightly pink inside. Remove from heat and stir in the vinegar and mustard, with salt and pepper to taste.

2 Arrange the salad greens on 4 individual serving plates.

3 Spoon the hot chicken liver mixture on top of the salad greens and sprinkle with the scallions and parsley sprigs. Serve immediately.

2 tablespoons butter

5 tablespoons light olive oil

1 lb. chicken livers, cut in half

2 tablespoons red wine vinegar

1 teaspoon wholegrain mustard

8 oz. mixed salad greens (e.g. red oakleaf, chicory, radicchio, endive, escarole)

2 scallions, thinly sliced

flat-leaf parsley sprigs

salt and pepper

Serves 4
Preparation time: 20 minutes
Cooking time: about 5 minutes

hot chicken liver salad

charbroiled chicken with tomato-chile salsa

1 Put the chicken breasts on a board, cover with wax paper, and pound with a rolling pin to flatten slightly. Remove the paper and place the chicken in a shallow dish. Whisk together the olive oil, lime zest and juice, and pepper to taste. Brush over the chicken, then cover and marinate at room temperature for about 1 hour.

2 To make the salsa, put all the ingredients in a bowl, along with salt and pepper to taste, and mix well. Cover and chill until ready to serve.

3 Brush a little of the oil from the chicken on a griddle pan and place over medium heat until hot. Put the chicken breasts and the remaining oil on the pan and cook for 3–5 minutes on each side, or until the chicken feels tender when pierced with a skewer or fork.

4 Serve the chicken on a bed of salad greens, garnished with lime wedges and cilantro sprigs. Serve the salsa on top.

■ Chiles vary enormously in their 'hotness', but generally, the smaller they are, the hotter they will be.

2 large boneless, skinless, chicken breasts

¼ cup extra virgin olive oil

finely grated zest and juice of 2 limes

salt and pepper

mixed salad greens, for serving

Tomato-Chile Salsa:

½ lb. cherry tomatoes, quartered lengthwise (about 1½ cups)

1–2 fresh red or green chiles, seeded and very finely diced

2 garlic cloves, crushed

3 tablespoons extra virgin olive oil

juice of 1 lime

2 tablespoons chopped cilantro

½ teaspoon sugar

For Garnishing:

lime wedges

cilantro sprigs

Serves 2

Preparation time: 15 minutes, plus marinating

Cooking time: about 10 minutes

12 oz. dried penne, conchiglie, or gnocchi

Sauce:

2 tablespoons olive oil

½ lb. boneless, skinless, chicken breasts, diced

1 large onion, finely chopped

3 celery stalks, diced

2 carrots, diced

2 teaspoons dried oregano

½ cup red wine

15 oz. can chopped tomatoes

salt and pepper

For Garnishing:

1 tablespoon oregano leaves

Parmesan shavings

1 To make the sauce, heat the oil in a frying pan and fry the chicken pieces, stirring occasionally, until lightly colored. Add the onion, celery, and carrots, and cook for 5 minutes until softened.

2 Add the oregano, wine, and tomatoes, and season to taste with salt and pepper. Bring the sauce to a boil, cover the pan, and simmer for 10 minutes.

3 Meanwhile, cook the pasta in lightly salted boiling water according to package instructions or until just tender. Drain, and toss with half of the sauce. Transfer the pasta to a warmed serving dish, spoon the remaining sauce over it, and serve immediately, garnished with oregano leaves and Parmesan shavings.

Serves 4–6	
Preparation time: 10 minutes	
Cooking time: 20 minutes	

chicken & tomato pasta

chicken & orange shells

1 Put the chicken, orange zest and juice, the egg yolk, cream, and cayenne into a food processor with salt and pepper to taste, and blend for 1 minute or until smooth. Whisk the egg white in a grease-free bowl until firm peaks form, then fold it into the chicken mixture.

2 Spoon a little of the filling into each pasta shell. Arrange the shells over the bottom of a steamer and steam for 15 minutes or until the chicken filling has set.

3 Divide the salad greens among four serving plates and place the shells on top. Drizzle with the olive oil and garnish with the fennel sprigs and basil leaves.

½ lb. cooked, boneless, skinless, chicken breasts, roughly chopped

grated zest of 1 orange

2 tablespoons orange juice

1 egg, separated

3 tablespoons heavy cream

½ teaspoon cayenne pepper

16 large dried pasta shells, cooked

1 bag of mixed salad greens

¼ cup olive oil

salt and pepper

For Garnishing:

fennel sprigs

basil leaves

Serves 4
Preparation time: 10 minutes
Cooking time: 15 minutes

1 Bring a large pot of water to a boil. Add ½ tablespoon of the oil and a generous pinch of salt. Cook the pasta shells for 8–12 minutes until just tender.

2 Heat the remaining oil in a large frying pan, add the chicken, and sauté gently for 2 minutes. Stir in the peas, garlic, basil, thyme, parsley, and red pepper, and cook, stirring, for a further 2 minutes.

3 Pour the chicken mixture into a large greased ovenproof dish, add the pasta shells, season with salt and pepper, and toss well. Sprinkle with the grated Parmesan and bake in a preheated oven at 400°F for 20 minutes. Garnish with basil sprigs and serve immediately.

1½ tablespoons olive oil

10 oz. dried pasta shells or other pasta shapes

½ lb. cooked chicken breast, sliced into strips

1 cup fresh peas

1 garlic clove, crushed

2 tablespoons torn basil leaves

1 tablespoon chopped thyme

3 tablespoons chopped parsley

½ small red bell pepper, cored, seeded, and chopped

1 cup freshly grated Parmesan cheese

salt and pepper

basil sprigs, for garnishing

Serves 4

Preparation time: 10 minutes

Cooking time: about 35 minutes

chicken & pea pasta bake

pasta with chicken, cream, & mushroom sauce

1 Put the chicken in a pan with the onion, carrot, bouquet garni, and peppercorns. Add the water and add the sherry, if using. Bring to a boil, then lower the heat, cover, and poach the chicken for about 20 minutes until just tender when pierced with a fork.

2 Meanwhile, melt the butter in a separate pan, add the mushrooms, garlic, rosemary, and salt and pepper to taste, and sauté over medium heat, stirring constantly, for 5 minutes or until the mushrooms give up thin liquid. Remove from heat and, using a slotted spoon, transfer the mushrooms to a bowl, leaving the mushroom juices in the pan.

3 Bring a large pot of water to a boil. Add the oil and a generous pinch of salt. Cook the pasta for 8–12 minutes, or according to package instructions, until just tender.

4 Meanwhile, lift the chicken out of the poaching liquid, then strain the liquid into a bowl. Cut the chicken into strips, discarding the skin and bones.

5 Return the pan with mushroom juices to the heat, sprinkle in the flour, and cook for 1–2 minutes, stirring. Add the chicken poaching liquid a little at a time, beating well after each addition.

6 Bring to a boil, stirring. Lower the heat and stir in the cream. Add the chicken, mushrooms, and salt and pepper. Mix well, then simmer, stirring, for 5 minutes or until thickened.

7 Drain the pasta and turn into a warmed serving bowl. Pour in the sauce and toss to mix with the pasta. Serve hot, garnished with rosemary.

3 part-boned chicken breasts

1 small onion, quartered

1 carrot, roughly chopped

1 bouquet garni

a few black peppercorns

1¼ cups water

2 tablespoons dry sherry (optional)

½ stick (¼ cup) butter

½ lb. white mushrooms, thinly sliced (about 2⅓ cups)

2 garlic cloves, crushed

1 teaspoon chopped rosemary

1 teaspoon virgin olive oil

12 oz. dried pasta shapes (e.g. bows, penne, spirals)

1½ tablespoons flour

⅔ cup heavy cream

salt and pepper

rosemary sprigs, for garnishing

Serves 4
Preparation time: 30 minutes
Cooking time: about 30 minutes

■ Use white button mushrooms for this sauce as dark ones will spoil its delicate appearance.

chicken with scallions, soy, & celery

1 Place the chicken in a bowl. Add the salt, egg white, and cornstarch and mix thoroughly.

2 Heat the oil in a wok or large frying pan and add the chicken. Stir-fry over medium heat until the chicken is lightly and evenly browned. Remove the chicken with a slotted spoon and set aside on a plate.

3 Increase the heat and, when the oil is very hot, add the ginger and scallions, followed by the celery and green pepper. Stir-fry for about 30 seconds over high heat.

4 Return the chicken strips to the wok, along with the soy sauce and sherry. Mix well, and cook for a further 1–1½ minutes, stirring all the time. Transfer to a warmed serving dish and serve immediately.

½ lb. boneless, skinless, chicken breasts, cut into strips ½ x 3 inches

½ teaspoon salt

1 egg white

1 tablespoon cornstarch

¼ cup vegetable oil

4 slices of fresh ginger, peeled and cut into thin strips

2 scallions, cut into thin strips

1 small celery stalk, cut into strips

1 green bell pepper, cored, seeded, and cut into thin strips

2 tablespoons soy sauce

1 tablespoon dry sherry

Serves 3–4

Preparation time: 15 minutes

Cooking time: 7–8 minutes

1 Cut four pieces of foil 12 inches square. Cut three slits in each chicken breast and arrange on the foil.

2 Mix together the vegetable oil, lemon juice, thyme, and salt and pepper. Pull the foil up around the chicken, pour the sauce over the chicken, and seal the foil.

3 Cook the wrapped chicken under a preheated medium broiler, turning once, for 30 minutes until the juices run clear when pierced with a skewer.

4 Open the wrapped chicken, arrange the ham, cheese, and then tomatoes on the chicken breasts, and spoon a little sauce on the top. Broil the topping under high heat for 3–4 minutes until the cheese melts. Serve immediately.

4 boneless, skinless chicken breasts

¼ cup vegetable oil

1 tablespoon lemon juice

1 tablespoon dried thyme

4 oz. cooked ham, thinly sliced (about 4 slices)

2 oz. Gruyère cheese, thinly sliced (enough to cover 4 chicken breasts)

2 large tomatoes, sliced

salt and pepper

Serves 4

Preparation time: 5 minutes

Cooking time: 35 minutes

broiled chicken with cheese

warm salad of chicken & red pepper

1 Heat the oil in a large frying pan, add the chicken strips and red pepper, and fry, stirring frequently, for 10 minutes or until tender.

2 Whisk the dressing ingredients until thickened. Tear the lettuce leaves and put in a large salad bowl.

3 When the chicken and pepper strips are tender, remove them with a slotted spoon and place on top of the lettuce.

4 Pour the dressing into the pan, increase the heat to high, and stir until sizzling. Pour the hot dressing over the salad and toss to combine. Serve immediately, accompanied by good, crusty, French bread.

2 tablespoons extra virgin olive oil

1 lb. chicken breast fillets, cut diagonally into thin strips

1 red bell pepper, cored, seeded, and cut lengthwise into thin strips

2 small heads of lettuce, leaves separated

Dressing:

3 tablespoons extra virgin olive oil

2 tablespoons lemon juice

1 garlic clove, crushed

1 teaspoon Dijon mustard

salt and pepper

| **Serves** 4 |
| **Preparation time:** 10 minutes |
| **Cooking time:** 10 minutes |

spicy chicken braised with coconut juice ●

hot & sour chicken soup ●

tex-mex chicken with salsa ●

irish chicken fricassée ●

balti chicken ●

jamaican jerked chicken ●

chicken couscous ●

pollo alla cacciatora ●

burmese chicken curry & cellophane noodles ●

moroccan tagine ●

caribbean curry ●

italian roast chicken ●

spanish paella ●

good luck chicken ●

jambalaya ●

ginger chicken with honey ●

coast to coast

2 tablespoons oil

a 2-lb. chicken, cut into serving pieces

1 tablespoon Chinese wine or dry sherry

2 tablespoons soy sauce

2 onions, cut into quarters

3 scallions, chopped

3 garlic cloves, chopped

2 tablespoons curry paste

2 teaspoons curry powder

1¼ cups water

3 potatoes, cut into 1-inch pieces

2 carrots, cut into 1-inch pieces

¼ cup coconut juice

2 tablespoons flour

2 teaspoons sugar

salt and pepper

a few strips of green bell pepper, for garnishing

1 Heat 1 tablespoon of the oil in a wok or large frying pan. Add the chicken and stir-fry until browned. Add the wine or sherry, soy sauce, and salt and pepper. Stir-fry for a few seconds, then add the onions. Stir-fry for 30 seconds, then transfer to a pot.

2 Heat the remaining oil in the pan. Add the scallions and garlic, then the curry paste and powder. Stir-fry for 30 seconds, then add the water. Pour this over the chicken, and add the potatoes and carrots. Bring to a boil, cover, and simmer for 20 minutes, or until the chicken is tender. Mix the coconut juice with the flour and sugar, and stir into the pot. Cook until the sauce is thickened. Serve, garnished with strips of pepper.

Serves 4	
Preparation time: 15 minutes	
Cooking time: 30–40 minutes	

spicy chicken braised with coconut juice

1 Cover the dried shiitake mushrooms in warm water and let soak for about 20 minutes. Drain, and reserve the soaking liquid. Thinly slice the reconstituted mushrooms.

2 Bring the stock to a boil in a large pot over medium heat. Add the reserved mushroom liquid, the soy sauce, rice wine or sherry, the sugar, chile, and ginger. Lower the heat, add the mushrooms, and simmer for 20 minutes.

3 Add the shredded chicken, scallions, and carrots, and simmer for a further 5 minutes. Add salt and pepper to taste and serve hot, garnished with cilantro, if you like.

½ cup dried shiitake mushrooms

2 quarts Chicken Stock (see page 9)

2 tablespoons soy sauce

2 tablespoons Chinese rice wine or dry sherry

1 teaspoon soft brown sugar

1 fresh green chile, seeded and very finely chopped

2-inch piece of fresh ginger root, peeled and very finely shredded

½ lb. cooked, boneless, skinless, chicken, finely shredded

6 scallions, finely shredded

2 carrots, grated

salt and pepper

cilantro, for garnishing (optional)

Serves 4–6

Preparation time: 10 minutes, plus soaking

Cooking time: about 30 minutes

hot & sour chicken soup

tex-mex chicken with salsa

1 Score the chicken breasts diagonally in several places with a sharp knife. Whisk together the olive oil, lime zest and juice, and the cumin. Brush this over the chicken, working it into the incisions in the flesh. Cover, and marinate for about 1 hour.

2 To make the salsa, put all the ingredients into a bowl and stir well to mix. Cover, and chill until ready to serve.

3 Remove the chicken from the marinade, reserving the marinade. Put the chicken under a preheated hot broiler, or over a barbecue, and brush frequently with the marinade. Cook for 5–7 minutes on each side or until the chicken feels tender when pierced with a fork.

4 To serve, slice the chicken diagonally, along the lines of the first incisions. Arrange alongside the salsa on warmed plates. Serve immediately. Corn tortillas and avocado are the traditional accompaniments.

6 large boneless, skinless, chicken breasts

6 tablespoons extra virgin olive oil

finely grated zest and juice of 2 limes

¾ teaspoon ground cumin

Salsa:

1 lb. ripe tomatoes, skinned, seeded, and finely chopped

1 small onion, finely chopped

2 garlic cloves, crushed

1 hot green chile, seeded, and finely chopped

3 tablespoons extra virgin olive oil

2 teaspoons wine vinegar

juice of 1 lime

¼ teaspoon salt

Serves 6

Preparation time: 15 minutes, plus marinating

Cooking time: 10–15 minutes

irish chicken fricassée

1 To make the sauce, melt the butter in a saucepan, stir in the flour, and gradually add the stock and milk until blended. Bring to a boil, stirring constantly until thick and smooth, and then cook for a few minutes.

2 Mix the egg yolk and cream, and whisk into the sauce along with the remaining ingredients. Fold in the chicken strips, stir in the mushrooms and onions, and heat thoroughly.

3 Serve the chicken fricassée on a large flat dish garnished with the bacon rolls, lemon wedges, and a dusting of paprika.

1½ lbs. cooked, boneless, skinless, chicken breasts, cut into thick strips

1¾ cups white mushrooms, fried

16 pearl onions, peeled and blanched

Sauce:

½ stick (¼ cup) butter

½ cup flour

1¼ cups Chicken Stock (see page 9)

1¼ cups milk

1 egg yolk

⅓ cup heavy cream

1–2 tablespoons Worcestershire sauce

1 tablespoon mustard

1 teaspoon anchovy sauce

2 teaspoons capers

2 tablespoons finely chopped parsley

salt and pepper

For Garnishing:

8 strips of bacon, cut in half, rolled, and broiled

4 lemon wedges

paprika

Serves 4–6	
Preparation time: 20 minutes	
Cooking time: 10–15 minutes	

balti chicken

1 Dry-fry the peppercorns and fennel seeds in a wok or large frying pan over gentle heat, stirring constantly, for 2–3 minutes until fragrant. Remove, then pound to a fine powder using a mortar and pestle. Heat the oil in the same pan, add the onion, ginger, and garlic, and fry gently, stirring frequently, for about 5 minutes until soft but not brown.

2 Add the dry-fried powdered spices, garam masala, coriander, cumin, chili, and turmeric. Stir-fry this for 2–3 minutes, then add the coconut milk, lemon juice, and ½ teaspoon salt. Bring to a boil, stirring, then add the cardamoms, cinnamon, and bay leaf. Simmer, stirring occasionally, for about 15–20 minutes, until a glaze forms on the liquid.

3 Add the chicken, tomatoes, and sugar, and stir well. Cover, and cook over gentle heat for about 40 minutes, stirring occasionally, or until the chicken feels tender when pierced with a fork.

4 Discard the bay leaf and cinnamon stick, then taste, and add more salt if necessary. Serve hot, sprinkled with cilantro, and accompanied by some Indian bread.

½ teaspoon black peppercorns

½ teaspoon fennel seeds

2 tablespoons oil

1 onion, thinly sliced

1-inch piece of fresh ginger, peeled and crushed

1 garlic clove, crushed

1 tablespoon garam masala

1 teaspoon ground coriander

1 teaspoon ground cumin

1 teaspoon chili powder, or to taste

1 teaspoon turmeric

2 cups coconut milk

1 tablespoon lemon juice

6 cardamon pods, bruised

2-inch cinnamon stick

1 bay leaf

2 lbs. boneless, skinless, chicken thighs, cut into bite-sized pieces

4 ripe tomatoes, skinned, seeded, and roughly chopped

¼ teaspoon sugar

salt

cilantro, for garnishing

Serves 4–6

Preparation time: 30 minutes

Cooking time: about 1 hour

6 chicken joints

Jerked Seasoning:

⅓ cup allspice berries

2-inch cinnamon stick

1 teaspoon freshly grated nutmeg

1 fresh red chile, seeded and finely chopped

4 scallions, thinly sliced

1 bay leaf, crumbled

1 tablespoon dark rum

salt and pepper

Pineapple Chutney:

2 fresh pineapples, peeled and chopped

1-inch piece of fresh ginger, peeled and finely chopped

1 onion, finely chopped

1 fresh red chile, seeded and finely chopped

½ cup vinegar

generous cup soft dark brown sugar

Serves 6

Preparation time: 20 minutes, plus marinating

Cooking time: 30–40 minutes

1 First make the jerked seasoning. Pound the allspice berries, cinnamon, and nutmeg using a mortar and pestle. Add the chile, scallions, bay leaf, and salt and pepper to the mortar, and pound to a thick paste. Stir the rum into the paste and mix well. Slash the chicken deeply on the skin side 2–3 times, and then rub the paste all over the chicken. Cover and marinate for 1–2 hours.

2 Meanwhile, make the pineapple chutney. Put all the ingredients into a saucepan and stir well. Place over medium heat and stir until the sugar has completely dissolved. Bring to a boil and then reduce the heat a little. Cook vigorously, stirring occasionally, until the chutney thickens.

3 Pour the chutney into sterilized glass jars and seal. If you like, it can be made in advance and kept for 2–3 weeks in a refrigerator.

4 Put the jerked chicken into a roasting pan and roast in a preheated oven at 400°F for 20–30 minutes, or cook under a preheated hot broiler. Serve with the pineapple chutney and some plain boiled rice.

jamaican jerked chicken

chicken couscous

1 Heat the oil in a pot and quickly fry the onions, garlic, and spices. Stir in the tomato paste and chickpeas, and season to taste. Cover with water and bring to a boil. Simmer, stirring often, for 1 hour. Top up with water to cover the chickpeas.

2 Add the chicken pieces, cover, and simmer for 20 minutes, stirring occasionally. Stir the carrots, parsnips, and potatoes into the chicken and chickpeas, cover with water, and bring to a boil. Put the couscous into a bowl and cover with boiling water. Add the cinnamon and orange flower water and stir.

3 Put the couscous and half the butter in a steamer on top of the pot. Cover and cook for 30 minutes, adding the zucchini and raisins halfway through. Remove the couscous from the steamer and fork through it the remaining butter. Serve the chicken and vegetables on the couscous, and garnish with cilantro.

2 tablespoons virgin olive oil

2 onions, finely chopped

3 garlic cloves, finely chopped

2 teaspoons ground coriander

2 teaspoons cumin

2 teaspoons ground turmeric

2 teaspoons chili powder

2 tablespoons tomato paste

¾ cup dried chickpeas already soaked

12 boneless, skinless, chicken thighs, cut into large bite-sized pieces

4 carrots, thickly sliced

2 parsnips, thickly sliced

2 potatoes, cut into chunks

1 lb. couscous (2⅔ cups)

½ teaspoon ground cinnamon

a few drops of orange flower water

½ stick (¼ cup) butter

4 zucchini, thickly sliced

2 tablespoons golden raisins

salt and pepper

cilantro, for garnishing

Serves 6–8

Preparation time: 40 minutes, plus soaking

Cooking time: about 2 hours

pollo alla cacciatora

1 Soak the dried mushrooms in the warm water for 20 minutes.

2 Meanwhile, heat the oil in a large frying pan or chicken fryer, add the chicken, and sauté over medium heat for 7–10 minutes, until golden on all sides. Remove with a slotted spoon and set aside on a plate.

3 Add the onion, carrot, celery, and garlic to the pan and gently fry, stirring frequently, for about 7–10 minutes until softened. Drain the mushrooms and reserve the soaking liquid. Finely chop the mushrooms and add them to the pan, along with the reserved liquid and the wine. Increase the heat and stir until bubbling. Add the tomatoes with their juice, tomato paste, herbs, sugar, and salt and pepper.

4 Return the chicken and juices to the pan. Cover, and simmer over gentle heat, stirring occasionally, for 40 minutes or until the chicken is tender when pierced with a fork. Adjust the seasoning to taste. Serve hot, sprinkled with chopped parsley.

■ Italian dried mushrooms – porcini – are available at most delicatessens and good supermarkets. Though expensive, they are full of flavor, so you need only a very small quantity.

½ oz. dried mushrooms (about ⅓–½ cup)

⅔ cup warm water

2 tablespoons extra virgin olive oil

4 skinless chicken portions

1 onion, finely chopped

1 large carrot, finely chopped

1 large celery stalk, finely chopped

2 garlic cloves, crushed

⅔ cup Italian white wine

15 oz. can peeled plum tomatoes, roughly chopped

1 tablespoon tomato paste

1 teaspoon dried oregano

1 teaspoon dried mixed herbs

large pinch of sugar

salt and pepper

chopped parsley, for garnishing

Serves 4

Preparation time: 20 minutes

Cooking time: about 1 hour

burmese chicken curry & cellophane noodles

1 To make the spice paste, put all the ingredients in a food processor or blender and blend to a thick paste.

2 Heat the peanut oil in a large heavy pot, add the spice paste, and fry over gentle heat, stirring constantly, for 5 minutes. Add the chicken pieces and fry, stirring constantly, for a further 5 minutes to seal. Stir in the chili powder, turmeric, salt, coconut milk, and stock. Bring to a boil, then reduce the heat and simmer very gently, stirring occasionally, for 30 minutes or until the chicken is tender.

3 Stir the coconut cream into the curry and then simmer over medium heat for 2–3 minutes, stirring constantly, until the coconut has dissolved and thickened the sauce slightly. Taste, and adjust the seasoning if necessary.

4 Drop the noodles into a pot of salted boiling water. Bring the water back to a boil and cook the noodles for 3 minutes. Drain the noodles, and toss them with a little sesame oil.

5 To serve, divide the noodles among 4 deep soup bowls, and ladle some chicken curry over each portion. Serve the accompaniments separately.

¼ cup peanut oil

1½ lbs. boneless, skinless, chicken breasts, cut into bite-sized pieces

1½ teaspoons chili powder

½ teaspoon ground turmeric

½ teaspoon salt

2½ cups coconut milk

1¼ cups Chicken Stock (see page 9)

¼ cup coconut cream

12 oz. cellophane noodles

sesame oil

salt and pepper

Spice Paste:

4 large garlic cloves, chopped

2 onions, chopped

1 red chile, seeded and chopped

1-inch piece of fresh ginger, peeled and chopped

1 teaspoon shrimp paste (optional)

Accompaniments:

3 scallions, sliced

2 tablespoons fried onion flakes

2 tablespoons cilantro

1 lemon, cut into wedges

Serves 4

Preparation time: 15 minutes

Cooking time: 50 minutes

1 Mix the turmeric, paprika, and cinnamon in a small bowl, and season with salt and pepper, then coat the chicken with it.

2 Heat the oil in a large frying pan or chicken fryer, and cook the chicken over medium heat, stirring constantly, for 5 minutes until it changes color. Remove the chicken pieces with a slotted spoon and set aside on a plate.

3 Add the onion, ginger, and garlic to the pan and cook over gentle heat, stirring frequently, for about 5 minutes until softened. Gradually stir in the chicken stock, increase the heat to high, and bring to a boil. Add the dried fruit and return the chicken and its juices to the pan. Mix well. Cover, and simmer, stirring occasionally, for 40 minutes until the chicken is tender when pierced with a skewer or fork. Adjust the seasoning to taste. Serve hot, with plain boiled rice.

2 teaspoons ground turmeric

2 teaspoons paprika

1 teaspoon ground cinnamon

12 boneless, skinless, chicken thighs, cut into bite-sized pieces

2 tablespoons extra virgin olive oil

1 onion, finely chopped

1-inch piece of fresh ginger, peeled and crushed

1 garlic clove, crushed

2½ cups Chicken Stock (see page 9)

8 oz. mixed dried fruit, e.g. prunes, apricots, apples, pears, peaches (about 1¼–1½ cups)

salt and pepper

Serves 4

Preparation time: 15 minutes

Cooking time: about 50 minutes

moroccan tagine

caribbean curry

1 Heat the oil in a heavy frying pan, add the chicken pieces and fry over medium heat until golden brown all over. Transfer to a large, heavy pot.

2 Add the onions, garlic, and chile to the frying pan and cook, stirring occasionally, over medium heat for about 5 minutes until the onions are soft. Add the curry powder, stir well, and cook for 3 minutes, stirring. Add the eggplant, chayote, papaya, and tomatoes, and cook for a further 2–3 minutes.

3 Put the curried mixture into the pot and add the chicken stock and coconut milk. Cover, and simmer for about 30 minutes, until the chicken is cooked and the vegetables are tender. Stir in the lime juice and rum or Madeira, and season with salt and pepper. Serve with plain boiled rice and fried bananas.

5 tablespoons peanut oil

a 4-lb. chicken, cut into 6–8 serving pieces

2 onions, finely chopped

1 garlic clove, crushed

1 fresh red chile, seeded and finely chopped

2 tablespoons curry powder

1 small-to-medium eggplant, peeled and cubed

1 chayote (see below), peeled and cubed

1 unripe papaya, peeled and sliced

2 tomatoes, skinned and chopped

⅔ cup Chicken Stock (see page 9)

⅔ cup coconut milk

2 tablespoons lime juice

1 tablespoon rum or Madeira

salt and pepper

Serves 4–6

Preparation time: 10 minutes

Cooking time: 50 minutes

■ Chayotes are pale green, pear-shaped vegetables from the Caribbean. They can be found in large supermarkets or ethnic stores.

1 Melt the butter in a heavy saucepan, chop the chicken giblets, and add them to the pan. Fry gently for 10 minutes.

2 Add the breadcrumbs and fry until browned, then add the chopped tomatoes and simmer for 10 minutes. Remove from heat and let cool.

3 Add the egg to the mixture along with the cheese, milk, cream, and salt and pepper to taste, and mix thoroughly. Stuff the chicken with the mixture, putting the hard-boiled egg in the center. Sew the opening securely closed with kitchen string or thread.

4 Place the chicken in an oiled roasting pan, pour the olive oil over it, sprinkle with salt and pepper, and roast in a preheated oven at 400°F for 1½ hours or until the chicken is tender. Serve immediately.

2 tablespoons butter

a 3-lb. roasting chicken, with giblets

1¼ cups dry breadcrumbs

3 tomatoes, skinned and chopped

1 egg, beaten

4 oz. Romano cheese, grated (about 2 cups)

½ cup milk

¼ cup light cream

1 hard-boiled egg

¼ cup olive oil

salt and pepper

Serves 6

Preparation time: 30 minutes

Cooking time: 1½–2 hours

italian roast chicken

spanish paella

1 Scrub the mussels with a small stiff brush and scrape off the beards and the barnacles with a small sharp knife. Discard any open mussels.

2 Slice 2 garlic cloves and crush the remainder. Put the slices into a large pot, along with the herbs, wine, ⅔ cup of the stock, and salt and pepper. Add the mussels, cover, and bring to a boil. Shake the pot, and simmer for 5 minutes until they open. Remove the mussels and set aside, discarding any which remain closed. Strain the liquid and set aside.

3 Heat half of the oil and sauté the squid for 5 minutes, stirring. Add the onion, red pepper, and crushed garlic, and cook, stirring, for 5 minutes. Add the mussel cooking liquid, tomatoes, and salt and pepper. Bring to a boil stirring, then simmer, stirring, for 15–20 minutes. Transfer to a bowl.

4 Heat the remaining oil in the pot and sauté the chicken for 5 minutes. Add the rice, and stir briefly. Stir in the squid mixture. Add one third of the remaining stock and bring to a boil, stirring. Boil for 3–4 minutes, cover, and simmer for 30 minutes. Add more stock as needed and stir, to cook evenly. Cook until the chicken and rice are tender and the liquid is absorbed.

5 Add the peas and shrimp and simmer, stirring, for 5 minutes, adding stock if needed. Add the mussels, cover with foil, and cook for 5 minutes. Serve immediately.

2 lbs. fresh mussels

4 garlic cloves

1 bunch of fresh mixed herbs

⅔ cup dry white wine

2 quarts Chicken Stock (see page 9)

¼ cup extra virgin olive oil

4 small squid, cleaned and sliced into rings

1 large onion, finely chopped

1 red bell pepper, cored, seeded, and chopped

4 large ripe tomatoes, skinned, seeded and chopped

12 skinless, boneless, chicken thighs, cut into bite-sized pieces

about 2⅔ cups short-grain rice (1 lb.)

1 cup fresh or frozen peas

12 raw jumbo shrimp, peeled, with tails left intact

salt and pepper

Serves 6

Preparation time: about 40 minutes

Cooking time: about 1¼ hours

good luck chicken

1 Heat the sesame oil in a pan and fry the chicken breasts for 10–15 minutes, turning occasionally. When cooked, drain, and sprinkle with the five-spice powder. Cut the chicken into julienne strips and stir in the bean sprouts. Cut the scallions into julienne strips, and add to the chicken mixture. Season with salt and pepper.

2 Cut the phyllo dough into twenty 4 x 7 inch rectangles. Spoon a little chicken mixture along the shorter edge of each one and sprinkle with soy sauce. Tuck the sides over the filling and roll the dough to enclose the filling. Mix the flour with a little water to make the paste, brush along the edge of the roll and press to seal.

3 Heat the oil in a wok or large frying pan and cook the rolls in batches for about 4–6 minutes. Drain on paper towels and serve at once.

1 tablespoon sesame oil

3 boneless, skinless, chicken breasts

2 teaspoons five-spice powder

2 cups bean sprouts

2 scallions

3 sheets of phyllo dough

soy sauce

2 teaspoons flour

water, to mix

sunflower oil, for deep-frying

salt and pepper

Makes about 20

Preparation time: 20 minutes

Cooking time: 20–25 minutes

jambalaya

1 Discard any open mussels. Put the wine, water, bouquet garni, garlic, mussels, and salt and pepper into a large pot. Cover and bring to a boil. Shake the pot and simmer for 5 minutes or until the mussels open. Remove from the liquid and set aside, discarding any which remain closed. Strain the liquid and set aside.

2 Heat the oil in a large, heavy pot. Fry the chicken and chorizo for 5 minutes. Remove and set aside. Add the onions, celery, and peppers, and fry for 5 minutes. Add the tomatoes, herbs, and cayenne, and stir. Add the mussel liquid and the stock. Bring to a boil, stirring. Add the rice, bay leaves, salt and pepper, and stir.

3 Return the chicken, chorizo, and juices to the pot, cover, and simmer for 40 minutes, adding stock as needed. Discard the bay leaves. Add the mussels to the chicken and rice, cover, and heat for 5 minutes, then serve.

1 lb. fresh mussels, scrubbed and debearded

⅔ cup dry white wine

⅔ cup water

1 bouquet garni

2 garlic cloves, crushed

2 tablespoons canola or vegetable oil

a 3-lb. roasting chicken, giblets removed, cut into 8 pieces

6 oz. chorizo sausage, chopped

2 onions, finely chopped

2 celery stalks, finely chopped

1 green bell pepper, cored, seeded, and chopped

1 red bell pepper, cored, seeded, and chopped

15 oz. can chopped tomatoes

1 teaspoon dried thyme

1 teaspoon dried oregano

1 teaspoon cayenne pepper

2½ cups hot Chicken Stock (see page 9)

about 2⅔ cups long-grain rice (1 lb.)

2 bay leaves, broken up

salt and pepper

Serves 6

Preparation time: 40 minutes

Cooking time: about 1 hour

chicken galantine ●

chicken suprêmes with roast peppers ●

chicken with 40 garlic cloves ●

chicken & red pesto roulades ●

chicken with white wine, gruyère, & mushrooms ●

coq au vin ●

chicken with tomatoes & pimiento ●

chicken cannelloni ●

carnival chicken with sweet potato mash ●

spiced roast chicken ●

chicken foie gras ●

maple chicken with orange & watercress ●

chicken crêpes ●

entertaining

chicken galantine

1 To bone the chicken, set it on a cutting board breast-side down. Cut through the skin along the backbone from the neck to the tail. Be careful not to cut the skin from now on. Scrape the flesh away from the bones, gradually working around the carcass, breaking the legs and wings away from the rib cage as you go. Cut off the ends of the wing and leg joints, and pull out the rib cage. Remove the breastbone gently, being very careful not to tear the skin along the breastbone. Using a small knife, scrape the flesh from the leg and wing bones.

2 Spread out the boned bird on a work surface, skin-side down. Fold the legs and wings towards the inside. Trim the bird to a neat rectangular shape. Spread a sheet of wax paper over the flesh and gently flatten with a rolling pin.

3 Mix the bulk sausage and ground veal in a large bowl. Stir in the onion, green peppercorns, lemon zest and juice, and sherry. Season with pepper.

4 Spread the mixture over the inside of the chicken, and place the tongue on top. Mix the mushrooms, parsley, breadcrumbs, and capers. Season, and put the mixture over the tongue. Pull up the sides of the skin to enclose the filling, and fasten along the top with a skewer. Pull up the ends and sew with a needle and thread to make a neat rectangular shape. Weigh the roll.

a 4-lb. chicken

½ lb. bulk sausage

½ lb. ground veal

1 onion, finely chopped

1 tablespoon green peppercorns, drained

grated zest and juice of 1 lemon

2 tablespoons dry sherry

2 oz. tongue, sliced (about 3–4 slices)

a generous ½ cup finely chopped mushrooms

¼ cup finely chopped parsley

⅔ cup fresh white breadcrumbs

1 tablespoon capers, drained and chopped

2 tablespoons butter, melted

1 tablespoon oil

salt and pepper

holly or herb sprigs, for decoration

Serves 8–10

Preparation time: 1 hour

Cooking time: about 2½–2¾ hours

5 Place the roll on a large sheet of foil in a roasting pan. Brush all over with butter and oil, then seal the foil. Bake in a preheated oven at 350°F for 30 minutes per pound.

6 Open the foil, baste, and cook for a final 30 minutes until golden brown. To test if the galantine is cooked, insert a skewer – the juices should run clear. Remove from the foil and place on a wire rack to cool. Remove the threads. Slice thinly and decorate with holly or herb sprigs.

chicken &
red pesto
roulades

1 Make a long horizontal slit through the thickest part of each chicken breast without cutting right through.

2 Beat the butter and pesto in a bowl, then spread the mixture inside the cavities in the chicken breasts, dividing it equally between them. Close the chicken tightly around the pesto mixture. Stretch the bacon slices with the flat of a large knife blade, then wrap 2 bacon slices tightly around each chicken breast, overlapping them so that the chicken is completely enclosed in the bacon. Secure with toothpicks.

3 Heat the oil in a large frying pan, add the chicken roulades in a single layer, and sauté over medium heat for 3 minutes on each side, or until the bacon colors. Add the wine and stock, and bring to a boil, spooning liquid over the chicken constantly. Cover, and simmer gently for about 15 minutes until the chicken is tender when pierced with a fork.

4 Remove the roulades from the pan with a slotted spoon, cover, and keep warm. Add the cream or crème fraîche to the pan and boil, stirring, until the liquid has thickened and reduced to a syrupy glaze. Season to taste. Serve hot, with the sauce poured over and around the roulades. Garnish with cherry tomatoes and basil leaves.

6 large, boneless, skinless, chicken breasts

½ stick (¼ cup) butter

¼ cup red pesto

12 slices of Canadian bacon

2 tablespoons virgin olive oil

½ cup red wine

¾ cup hot Chicken Stock (see page 9)

¼ cup heavy cream or crème fraîche

salt and pepper

For Garnishing:

cherry tomatoes

fresh basil leaves

Serves 6
Preparation time: 20 minutes
Cooking time: 20–25 minutes

1 Put the chicken breasts in a single layer in an ovenproof dish, dot with half of the butter, sprinkle with the herbs, and season with salt and pepper. Cover with foil and place in a preheated oven at 350°F for 30 minutes or until just tender when pierced with a fork.

2 Meanwhile, melt the remaining butter in a saucepan, add the mushrooms, and sauté over medium heat, stirring often, for about 5 minutes. Sprinkle in the flour and cook, stirring, for 1–2 minutes. Remove the pan from the heat and add the milk gradually, beating with a whisk. Add the wine in the same way.

3 Return the pan to the heat and bring to a boil, stirring. Lower the heat and simmer, stirring, for about 5 minutes until thickened. Add the cream, two-thirds of the Gruyère, the nutmeg, and salt and pepper. Simmer over gentle heat for 5 minutes. Remove from heat.

4 When the chicken is tender, remove it from the oven and increase the oven temperature to high. Tip any chicken juices into the sauce and stir. Pour the sauce over the chicken and sprinkle with the remaining Gruyère. Return it to the oven and bake for about 5 minutes. Serve hot, with a salad, if you like.

4 part-boned chicken breasts, skinned

½ stick (¼ cup) sweet butter

½ teaspoon dried mixed herbs

½ teaspoon dried tarragon

½ lb. white mushrooms, thinly sliced (about 2⅓ cups)

¼ cup flour

1¼ cups milk

⅔ cup dry white wine

⅓ cup heavy cream

1 cup grated Gruyère or Swiss cheese

good pinch of freshly grated nutmeg

salt and pepper

Serves 4

Preparation time: 30 minutes

Cooking time: about 35 minutes

---

chicken with white wine, gruyère, & mushrooms

coq au vin

1 Rub the chicken with the dried thyme and pepper. Sauté half the pieces in the oil in a large flameproof casserole dish or large ovenproof pot, for 7–10 minutes until golden. Remove with a slotted spoon and set aside on a plate. Repeat with the remaining chicken. Add the bacon to the casserole dish and cook over medium heat, stirring frequently, until the fat runs. Add the onions, mushrooms, and garlic, and cook, stirring frequently, for 5 minutes.

2 Gently warm the brandy in a small saucepan. Return the chicken and its juices to the casserole dish, pour in the brandy, and ignite it with a taper. When the flames subside, add the wine and bring to a boil, stirring. Add the bouquet garni, and salt and pepper to taste. Cover, and simmer over gentle heat, stirring occasionally, for 40 minutes or until the chicken is tender.

3 Remove the chicken and vegetables to a warmed serving dish with a slotted spoon and keep hot. Discard the bouquet garni. Mix the butter and flour to a paste, and add to the sauce a little at a time until evenly blended. Bring to a boil and simmer, stirring, for 2–3 minutes until the sauce thickens. Season to taste.

4 Serve the chicken and vegetables with the sauce spooned over them, and garnish with thyme and parsley, if you like.

a 4-lb. roasting chicken, giblets removed, cut into 8 pieces

2 teaspoons dried thyme

3 tablespoons canola or other vegetable oil

6 oz. bacon, chopped

16 small pearl onions, peeled and blanched

½ lb. small white mushrooms (about ⅔ cups)

3 garlic cloves, crushed

3 tablespoons brandy

1½ cups red wine

1 bouquet garni

1 tablespoon butter

2 tablespoons flour

salt and pepper

For Garnishing:

thyme sprigs (optional)

parsley sprigs (optional)

Serves 4

Preparation time: 30 minutes

Cooking time: about 50 minutes

■ Serve this wonderful dish with a bottle of robust red wine, such as a Burgundy. This is the region in France where the original version of this dish was made famous.

chicken with tomatoes & pimiento

1 Heat the oil in a chicken fryer or large, heavy pot, add the onion and garlic, and cook gently for 15 minutes. Add the chicken pieces along with the pimiento, tomatoes, and salt and pepper to taste, and fry, turning, over medium heat until evenly browned.

2 Mix the tomato paste with a little lukewarm water, then stir it into the pot with the wine. Lower the heat, cover, and cook gently for 30 minutes.

3 Chop one of the rosemary sprigs and sprinkle it over the chicken. Cook for a further 30 minutes or until the chicken is tender, adding a little of the stock occasionally to keep it moist.

4 Serve the chicken hot, garnished with the remaining rosemary sprigs.

3–4 tablespoons olive oil

1 small onion, sliced

2 garlic cloves, crushed

a 2-lb. roasting chicken, cut into serving pieces

1 small pièce canned pimiento, chopped

4 tomatoes

1 tablespoon tomato paste

3–4 tablespoons dry white wine

a few rosemary sprigs

6–8 tablespoons Chicken Stock (see page 9)

salt and pepper

Serves 4
Preparation time: 20–30 minutes
Cooking time: 1½ hours

spiced roast chicken

1 Put the garlic, ginger, chiles and cumin seeds in a food processor or blender with half of the yogurt, the turmeric, mint, apple pie spice, and ½ teaspoon salt. Blend until all the ingredients are finely ground and evenly mixed into the yogurt – the mixture will be quite runny.

2 Slash the chicken skin through to the flesh with a sharp pointed knife, then tie with string. Put the bird into a large bowl and pour the yogurt mixture over it. Cover, and leave to marinate for at least 8 hours, turning the chicken from time to time.

3 Put the chicken into a casserole dish into which it just fits. Cook in a preheated oven at 350°F for 2–2¼ hours, or until the juices run clear when the thickest part of a thigh is pierced with a fork. Baste frequently, and halfway through the roasting time, spoon the remaining yogurt over the chicken.

4 Remove the bird from the oven, cover tightly with foil, and set aside to rest. Keep the cooking juices hot. Discard the string. Put the chicken on a warmed platter and pour the cooking juices over it. Garnish the chicken with mint sprigs. Serve with basmati rice and a dish of curried vegetables.

2 garlic cloves, roughly chopped

1-inch piece of fresh ginger, peeled and roughly chopped

1–2 dried red chiles, roughly chopped

1 tablespoon cumin seeds

1½ cups plain yogurt

2 teaspoons ground turmeric

1 teaspoon dried mint

½ teaspoon apple pie spice or pumpkin pie spice

a 4-lb. roasting chicken, giblets removed

salt

fresh mint sprigs, for garnishing

Serves 4

Preparation time: 15 minutes, plus marinating

Cooking time: 2–2¼ hours

■ In this Indian-inspired dish, the spiced yogurt forms a dark, crisp crust contrasting with the moist and succulent white meat.

chicken foie gras

1 Heat the oil and butter in a large frying pan, add the chicken, and sauté over medium heat for about 5 minutes until golden. Add the peppercorns and salt and pepper, then pour in the wine and water and stir to mix. Cover, and simmer gently for 15 minutes until the chicken is tender when pierced with a fork, turning it over and basting occasionally with the cooking liquid.

2 Meanwhile, mash the pâté in a bowl and gradually work in the cream until evenly mixed.

3 Remove the chicken from the pan with a slotted spoon, set aside, and keep warm.

4 Increase the heat and boil the cooking liquid for a few minutes until reduced, then add the pâté and cream mixture and stir until evenly mixed with the liquid in the pan. Let it bubble and thicken, then taste for seasoning.

5 Serve the chicken with the sauce poured over it, garnished with salad greens.

1 tablespoon canola or other vegetable oil

2 tablespoons sweet butter

6 boneless, skinless, chicken breasts

2 tablespoons pink peppercorns, crushed

1 cup rosé wine

1 cup water

4 oz. can pâté de foie gras

⅔ cup heavy cream

salt and pepper

salad greens, for garnishing

Serves 6

Preparation time: 10 minutes

Cooking time: about 25 minutes

1 Pierce the chicken legs at regular intervals with a skewer and put them into a shallow dish. Add the orange juice, onion, garlic, nutmeg, and salt and pepper to taste. Cover, and chill for 8 hours.

2 Lift the chicken legs out of the marinade with a slotted spoon, and place flesh-side down under a preheated moderate broiler and cook for 15 minutes. Turn them over, brush with maple syrup, and cook for a further 15–20 minutes until tender. Test the chicken by piercing the joints in the thickest part with a fork – if the juices run clear, not pink, the chicken is cooked.

3 While the chicken is cooking, make the salad. Grate the zest and squeeze the juice from 1 orange. Remove all the pith and peel from the remaining 3 oranges and divide into segments. Snip the watercress into sprigs. Put the orange segments and watercress into a serving dish and sprinkle with the onion. Mix the orange juice and zest with the oil and chives, and season with salt and pepper. Spoon the dressing over the salad and serve with the chicken.

maple chicken with orange & watercress

4 chicken legs

1 cup orange juice

1 onion, thinly sliced

1 garlic clove, crushed

freshly ground nutmeg

¼ cup maple syrup

salt and pepper

Salad:

4 thin-skinned oranges

1 bunch of watercress or small arugula or spinach leaves

1 small onion, finely chopped

¼ cup olive oil

2 tablespoons chopped chives

Serves 4	
Preparation time: 30 minutes, plus chilling	
Cooking time: 30–35 minutes	

chicken crêpes

1 First make the crêpe batter. Sift the flour into a bowl with a pinch of salt. Make a well in the center and pour in the egg. Add the milk, a little at a time, whisking and drawing in the flour from the sides of the well. Set aside to rest.

2 Meanwhile, melt half of the butter in a saucepan, add the onion and fry gently, stirring, for about 5 minutes or until softened. Add the mushrooms, increase the heat, and fry, stirring frequently, for 5 minutes or until the juices run. Remove from the heat and turn into a bowl. Stir in the chicken and the chopped parsley, and season with salt and pepper.

3 To cook the crêpes, whisk 1 tablespoon of the oil into the batter. Heat about 2 teaspoons of oil in a crêpe pan or frying pan until very hot. Pour in a small ladleful of batter, swirl it around the pan, and cook for about 1 minute until the crêpe is golden brown on the underside. Toss the crêpe and cook until golden brown on the other side, then tip out the crêpe so that the first side is underneath. Repeat with the remaining batter to make 12 crêpes in total, adding more oil as necessary. As the crêpes are made, stack them up.

4 To make the sauce, melt the remaining butter in a pan, sprinkle in the flour, and cook over medium heat, stirring, for 1–2 minutes. Remove the pan from the heat and slowly add 2 cups of the milk, beating after each addition. Return the pan to the heat and bring to a boil, stirring all the time. Lower the heat and simmer, stirring, for about 5 minutes until smooth. Remove the pan from the heat and pour about half the sauce into the chicken mixture. Fold gently to mix then taste for seasoning.

5 Put a good spoonful of filling in the center of each crêpe and roll up into a cigar shape. Stir the remaining milk and the cream into the remaining sauce in the pan, and season to taste. Return to the heat and beat until hot.

6 Pour one-third of the sauce into a casserole dish and spread evenly. Arrange the filled crêpes in a single layer in the dish, and pour the remaining sauce over them. Sprinkle with Parmesan. Place in a preheated oven at 375°F and cook for 20 minutes until bubbling. Serve hot with a salad.

½ stick (¼ cup) butter

1 small onion, very finely chopped

½ lb. white mushrooms, sliced (about 2⅓ cups)

½ lb. boneless, skinless, cooked chicken, shredded

3 tablespoons finely chopped parsley

¼ cup flour

2½ cups milk

⅔ cup heavy cream

salt and pepper

½ cup freshly grated Parmesan cheese

Crêpes:

1 cup flour

1 egg, beaten

1¼ cups milk

3–4 tablespoons canola or other vegetable oil

Serves 4–6
Preparation time: about 1 hour
Cooking time: 20 minutes

index